Learn the ABCs
Ff
Warren Rylands and
Samantha Nugent
LIGHTBOX
openlightbox.com

LIGHTBOX

Go to
www.openlightbox.com
and enter this book's
unique code.

ACCESS CODE

LBXA4898

Lightbox is an all-inclusive digital solution for the teaching and learning of curriculum topics in an original, groundbreaking way. Lightbox is based on National Curriculum Standards.

OPTIMIZED FOR

- ✔ TABLETS
- ✔ WHITEBOARDS
- ✔ COMPUTERS
- ✔ AND MUCH MORE!

STANDARD FEATURES OF LIGHTBOX

AUDIO High-quality narration using text-to-speech system

VIDEOS Embedded high-definition video clips

ACTIVITIES Printable PDFs that can be emailed and graded

WEBLINKS Curated links to external, child-safe resources

SLIDESHOWS Pictorial overviews of key concepts

INTERACTIVE MAPS Interactive maps and aerial satellite imagery

QUIZZES Ten multiple choice questions that are automatically graded and emailed for teacher assessment

KEY WORDS Matching key concepts to their definitions

VIDEOS

WEBLINKS

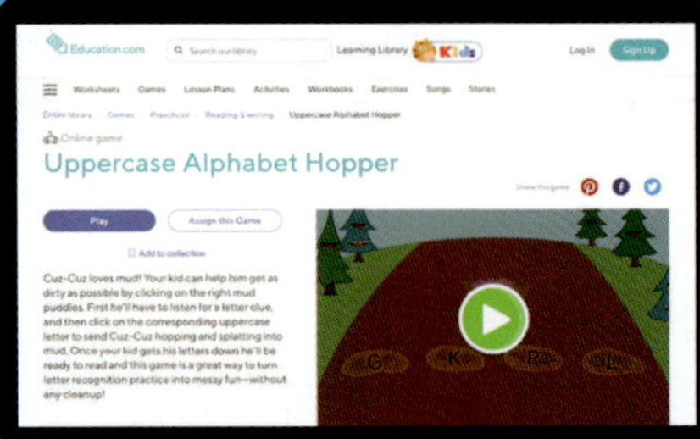

SLIDESHOWS

QUIZZES

This title is part of our Lightbox digital subscription

1-Year K–5 Subscription
ISBN 978-1-5105-5712-3

Access hundreds of Lightbox titles with our digital subscription.
Sign up for a **FREE** subscription trial at **www.openlightbox.com/trial**

Ff

CONTENTS

Let's discover the letter

This is an uppercase 

This is how you write it

This is a lowercase f

This is how you write it

The letter f can start many words.

fox
fruit
frog
forest

The letter f can be inside a word.

breakfast

muffin

traffic

surfer

wolf
The letter f
can be at the
end of a word.
reef
leaf

elf
windsurf

Many names start with an uppercase F.
Francis laughs.

Faith
is loud.

Freddie
plays
baseball.

Felix can
ride fast.

Floyd
likes
to read.

The letter f usually makes one sound.

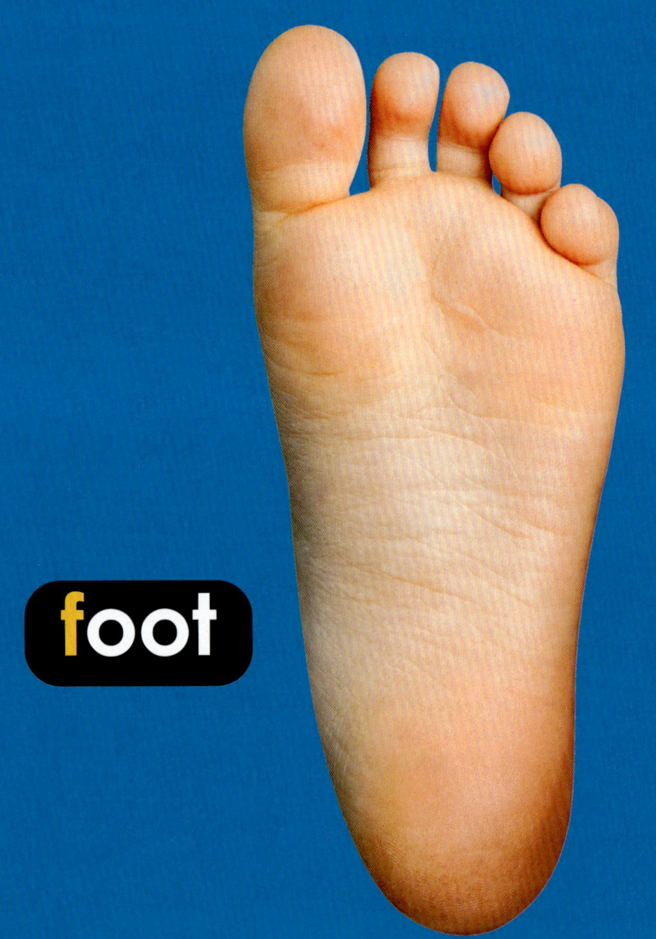

foot

waffle

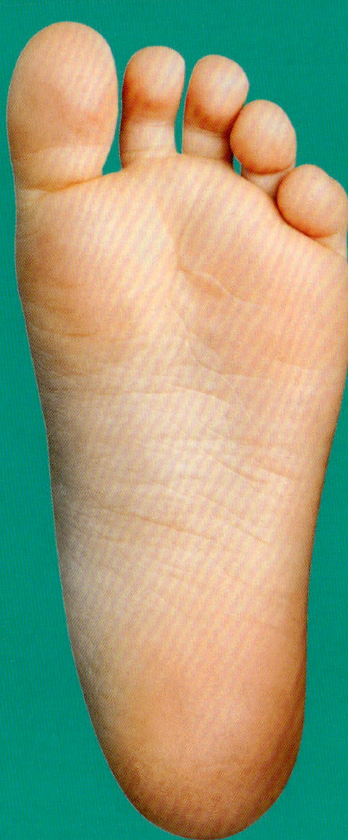

The letter f makes the f sound in the word **feet**.

The letter f makes the f sound in the word **waffle**.

Many words have an f sound.

family
before
four
after

When the letter f comes twice in a row, it makes only one f sound.

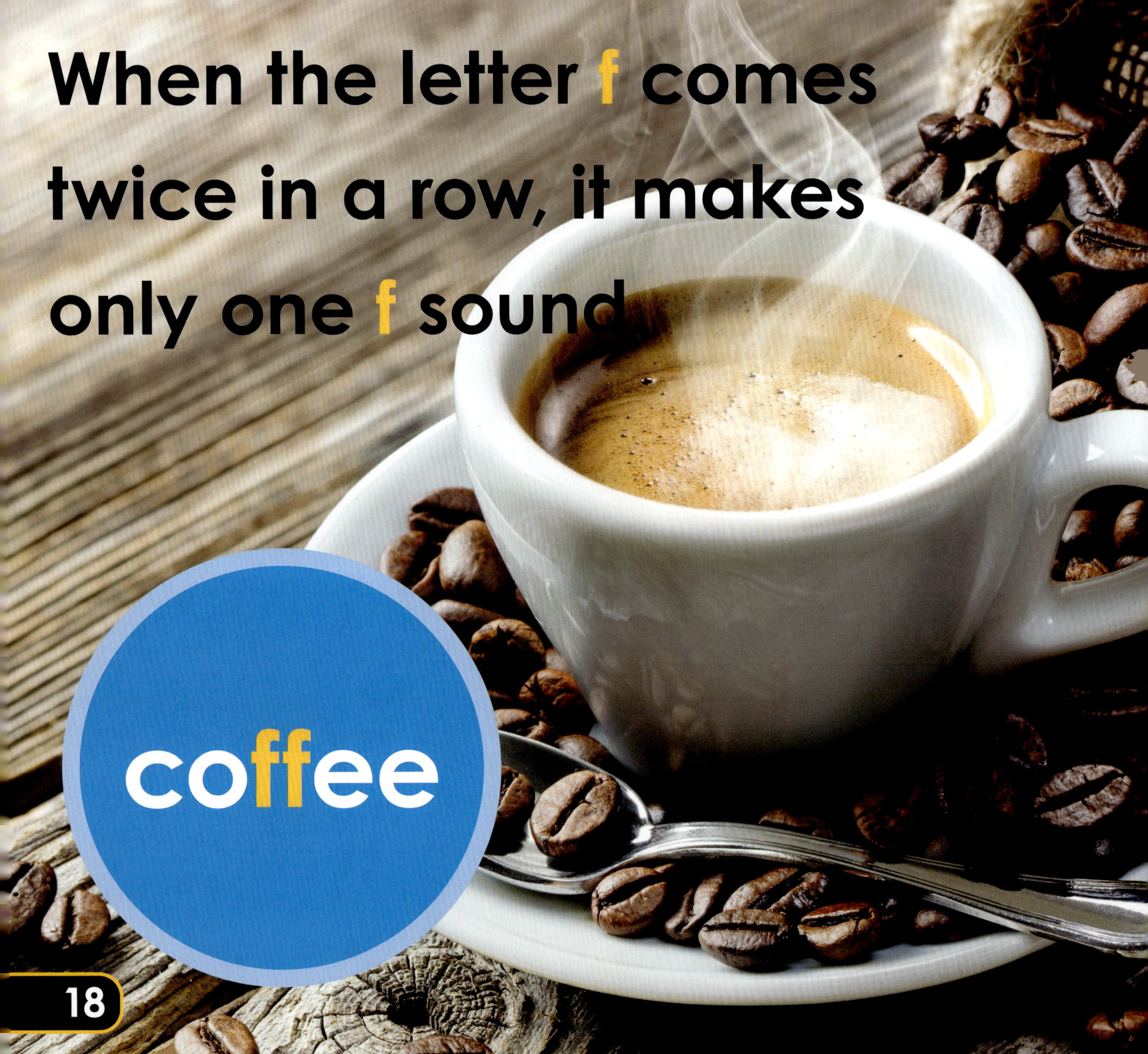

different
fluffy
off
stuff

Having Fun with F

Freddie was a surfer frog.

One Friday, he found a UFO by the reef.

Faith the wolf said it was a leaf.

Floyd the elf thought it was a fish.

Francis the buffalo believed it was fruit.

The four friends talked for hours.

Finally, they found it to be a muffin.

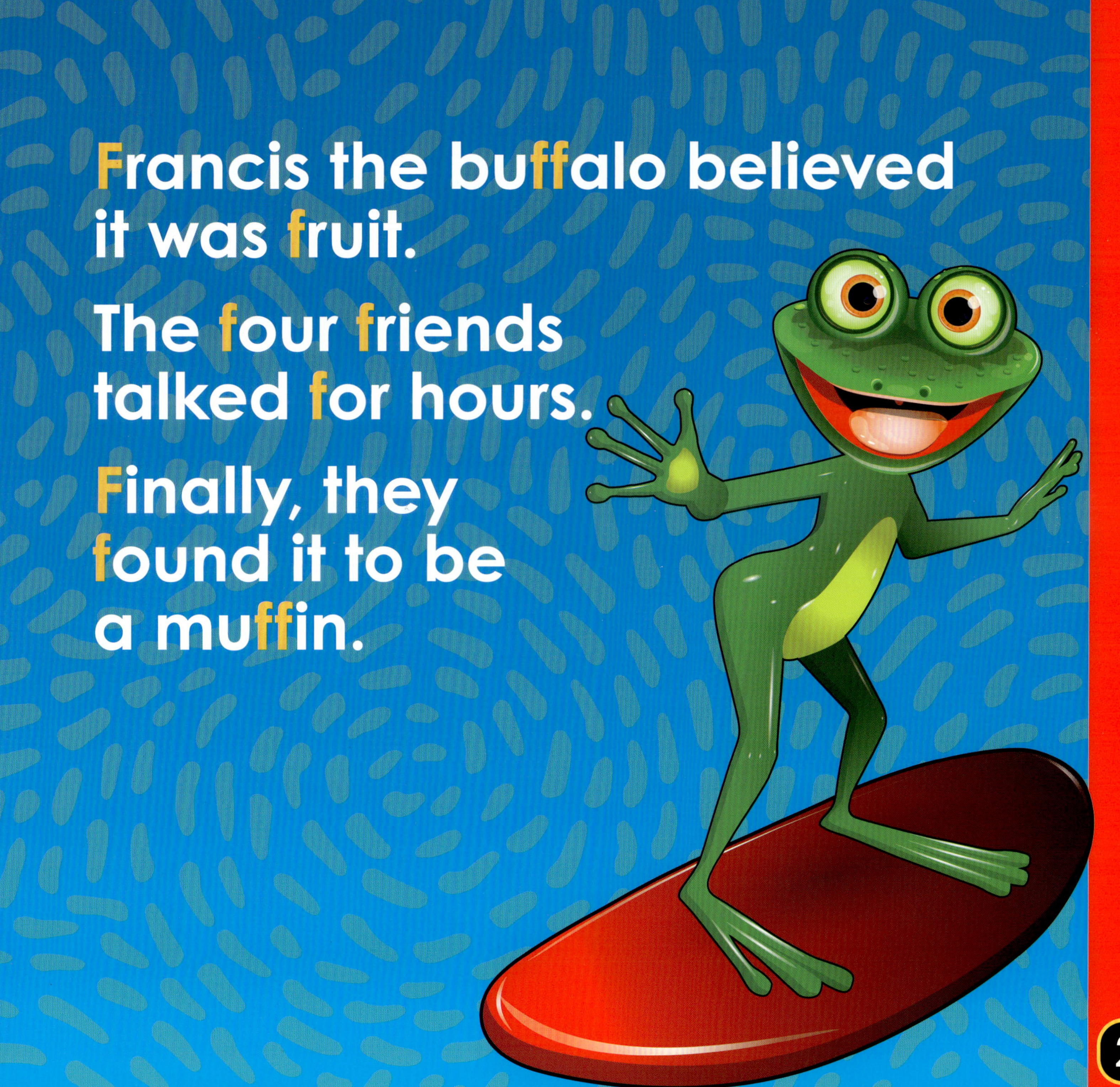

The alphabet has 26 letters.

F is the sixth letter in the alphabet.

Aa Bb Cc Dd Ee

Ff Gg Hh Ii Jj Kk

Ll Mm Nn Oo Pp

Qq Rr Ss Tt Uu Vv

Ww Xx Yy Zz

KEY WORDS

Research has shown that as much as 65 percent of all written material published in English is made up of 300 words. These 300 words cannot be taught using pictures or learned by sounding them out. They must be recognized by sight. This book contains 51 common sight words to help young readers improve their reading fluency and comprehension. This book also teaches young readers several important content words, such as proper nouns. These words are paired with pictures to aid in learning and improve understanding.

Page	Sight Words First Appearance
4	let, letter, the
5	a, an, how, is, it, this, write, you
6	can, farm, many, start, words
8	be
10	at, end, of
12	names, with
13	likes, plays, read, to
14	makes, one, sound
15	feet, in
16	face, have
17	after, before, family, four
18	comes, only, when
19	different, off
20	by, found, he, said, thought, was
21	for, they
22	has

Page	Content Words First Appearance
4	Ff
7	forest, fox, frog, fruit
8	breakfast, raft
9	muffin, surfer, traffic
10	leaf, reef, wolf
11	elf, windsurf
12	Francis
13	baseball, Faith, Felix, Floyd, Freddie
14	foot, waffle
18	coffee, row
19	stuff
20	fish, fun, UFO
20	friends, hours
22	alphabet

Published by Smartbook Media Inc.
276 5th Avenue, Suite 704 #917
New York, NY 10001
Website: www.openlightbox.com

Library of Congress Cataloging-in-Publication Data

Names: Rylands, Warren, author. | Nugent, Samantha, author.
Title: Ff / Warren Rylands and Samantha Nugent.
Description: New York, NY : Smartbook Media Inc., [2022] | Series: Learn the ABCs | Audience: Grades K-1
Identifiers: LCCN 2020054122 (print) | LCCN 2020054123 (ebook) | ISBN 9781510557505 (library binding) | ISBN 9781510557529 (ebook other)
Subjects: LCSH: English language--Consonants--Juvenile literature. | English language--Alphabet--Juvenile literature.
Classification: LCC PE1165 .R9526 2022 (print) | LCC PE1165 (ebook) | DDC 428/.13--dc23
LC record available at https://lccn.loc.gov/2020054122
LC ebook record available at https://lccn.loc.gov/2020054123

Printed in Guangzhou, China
1 2 3 4 5 6 7 8 9 0 25 24 23 22 21

022021
110820

Art Director: Terry Paulhus **Project Coordinator:** Sara Cucini

Every reasonable effort has been made to trace ownership and to obtain permission to reprint copyright material. The publisher would be pleased to have any errors or omissions brought to its attention so that they may be corrected in subsequent printings.

The publisher acknowledges Getty Images as the primary image supplier for this title.